Why You Can't Make Free Throws

The Mental, The Myth, and The Make

By Keith Coleman

Table of Contents

Preface

How much do you know about our military? How much thought do you give to what they do? Of course, we have our set times every year to pause and reflex on them for Memorial Day and Veterans Day. But their training is what is really the interesting part, here. Keith Coleman knows first-hand what it's like in the military, and the transformative power that it has.

Keith served 22 years in the Marine Corps. Of his 22 years, 9 of those years he worked with recruit training, more commonly known as boot camp. In the Marine Corps, boot camp lasts a total of 12 weeks. In those 12 weeks, a major transformation happens that turns young men and women into stronger, better, more capable adults. Have you ever wondered what happens in those 12 weeks that changes these recruits so much?

We are not only referring to how they dress wearing a uniform or their ability to remember a chain of command, but more so how they act and think. Yes, think. Keith has taken an interest in this phenomenon and has set out to uncover how so much change happen in such a short period of time. The simple answer lays in the mind.

What Keith discovered was that by changing the how the basics of the mind works, the recruits experience a major change in the way that they think and perceive. That's when he made the connection. If that is true with military training, then it must also be true for, well... any kind of training. He wondered to himself, "could this be used for basketball training, particularly in free throw shooting?" and set out to answer that question. This book is the result. It's the proof that the answer to that question is "yes".

This book shows how military recruit training can be used as a basis in teaching and improving free throwing in basketball players and provides real-world tips for making major improvements in players both on and off the court

the theory here is that military training can be used to help teach better free throw shooting.

The Three Components

Remember the big guy Shaquille O' Neal? Apart from him destroying anyone who dared take him on in the low post, he is much remembered for his poor free throw abilities. His career free throw success rate was only 52.7%. That roughly translates to only achieving 52 successful free throws for every one hundred attempts. That number is horrible, especially when you compare it to free throw greats such as Steve Nash at 90.43%, or Stephen Curry at 90.21%.

But Shaquille O'Neal is still thought of as one of the greats of basketball. So, if you don't need to be great at free throws to be great at the game, how does the free throw really even impact a game?

Though a free throw is just worth one point, one must not underestimate its importance. Despite the changing statistics season after season, a free throw is still around 33% more successful than a field goal. In a game where points dictate the winner, a free throw becomes an invaluable tool in every player's arsenal.

Think of it like this: it is very rare that you still make your shot when you are fouled. So, you already lost those two points that you could have made if only you were not fouled. If you miss both free throws, you just lost the opportunity to get those two points back. And this loss comes at a simple cost of one player's foul count. If you made your shot and you were fouled, you could have made a three-point play if you made that free throw shot.

This line of thinking posed several burning questions in my

head. For one, does the player's level of the playing have something to do with his free throw accuracy? What about his age?

Let's revisit Steve Nash. He has a high level of playing the game and he retired when he was 41. And yet he has retained the number one spot as the best free throw shooter to grace pro basketball. His age, we can theorize, did not have an impact on his free throw abilities. On a similar note, young Stephen Curry has a high level of ability and is currently holding the third spot for free throws.

Both young and old players can obtain high free throw performances. That must not be the factor.

This leaves us with the thought that a high level of ability may have an impact on a player's skills. But how about LeBron James? As one of the most explosive players in NBA history, his free throw accuracy is only at 74.4%. With a high level of skill like that, you would expect that he would have done better shooting from behind the line. So, if it's not playing at a high level that makes the difference either, what is going on?

According to Nash, practicing and sticking to a routine takes out a lot of the variable in a free throw. This is why he always took a practice shot without the ball before making the actual throw. He said that this helped him tap into his muscle memory and made it easier to make an accurate shot.

Now let us take a look at another free throw stat. Studies show that players do 5% worse on their first shot than the second one. This means that they are 5% less likely to make the first free throw shot than the second one. But this does not apply to Steve Nash, supposedly the best free throw shooter of all time until somebody from this generation beats his free throw record.

Steve Nash has a hitting average of 90% for the first shot and 91% on the second shot. People who tried to figure out why said that this is simply due to muscle memory. So, is the true culprit behind abysmal free throw rates muscle memory?

What needs to change in training that will transform the next generation of basketball players into skilled players both on and off the free throw line? What can make such an impact that it becomes the new standard of training the free throw for the next century or so?

In this book, you and I will explore together the many myths and truths surrounding free throws. You will learn what prevents you from making those free shots and you will gain valuable insights how to improve your free throw capabilities.

We will also go over the three components of what it takes to succeed in a free throw—physical, mental, and overall form. practice Primarily, we will delve deep into the mind of the free throw players, the myths surrounding free throw shots, and the mental ability required to succeed in it.

In the case of Shaq, there was no problem with his physical abilities. He was big and strong and can throw the ball from the free throw line. A lot of pundits argue that he could have improved by changing his throwing style, that he could have used the underhand shot, also known as granny style.

Or could it?

What free throw shooting techniques do I know now as a coach that I wish I knew as a player?

Is it muscle memory? Is it form? Or is it physical strength?

Join me in exploring a new technique and proven methods

of improving your free throw shots. Help your team, or yourself, become better at grabbing those free points behind the line.

I will also introduce you to my 10-20-70 rule. This rule is a culmination of my years of expertise in the field. Over the years, I have found out that the best approach to succeed behind the line is to focus 10% of your effort on the physical, 20% on your form, and 70% on mental agility and dexterity.

gratified theory

Introduction

Free throw shooting has become something of a lost art. Where everything else in basketball has been innovated, changed, and has progressed, the free throw capabilities of today's players from youth to pro have deteriorated. We have great sneakers designed perfectly for the court floor, to protect the ankle, and to give players the most out of their running and jumping. We have silky uniforms that allow for breathability and reduced drag. We have special wax for the floors. We have glass backboards and perfect netting. We've come a long, long way since James Naismith's basketball days. But our free throws haven't come with us.

The rate of success for free throws has hovered around 69% in men's college basketball since the 1960s, and since then the success rate has never gone higher than 70%. The NBA and WNBA have slightly higher rates with an average of 75% over fifty plus years of statistics. While 75% might seem decent, it's not. When you think of the mechanics of the free throw, the shot itself should be bulletproof. It's simple physics. Anybody who has played enough to be playing college-level ball should be hitting their free throws with almost perfect accuracy. But they're not. Nobody is.

The free throw is the one exception to the principle that athletes improve over time (within reason, of course). Every other part of a basketball player's game improves as he or she practices and rises through the levels of the sport. They run faster, pass more accurately, jump higher, score more baskets, defend better, and so on. But they don't improve on free throws. The average success rate of free throws has remained stagnant for over fifty years. It's insane!

According to Professor Ray Stefani*, a sports statistical analyst expert, improvement in athletics rides on any combination of the following four items: overall fitness level of an athlete, new technology, widespread coaching strategies, and innovative equipment. Because of these improvements over time both in individual athletes and in the sport itself, we're seeing records being broken consistently as the years go on. Runners are getting faster, swimmers are busting through records, football players can kick an accurate field-goal with their eyes covered and the ground shaking, it'd seem. So, why aren't these four factors doing anything to change free throw shooting rates?

For one, athlete performance in fitness doesn't seem to have an effect on free throws at all, so that knocks out the first option. Relative strength, for example, has no statistical connection to improved free throw rates (as is shown by the years that the WNBA had higher success rates than the NBA). So, we move to the second option: new technology. Well, none of the tech or equipment (the second and fourth options) has had innovation that would directly impact the free throw, either. That just leaves coaching.

Coaches have taught the same free throw technique since the dawn of the ball and the basket. The one-hand set up, shot straight out and up from the chest is still the norm. Coaches haven't changed their approach and haven't realized that they're at fault for their team's lacking ability to make free throw shots. Why have coaches and teams thrown the free-throw to the wayside?

Because the payoff isn't worth the problem solving

At least, to them it's not.

The free throw is an undervalued shot. Coaches would rather drill layups a million times a week and rely on play-making shots to win the game. If they can win like that, why would they take the time to address the lacking free throw success problem and work on complicated solutions when you can just avoid it all together? The logic seems sound. But did you know that the average basketball team misses between eight and ten free throws in a single game? That equates to an overall loss of 12 to 14 points, where the average margin of victory in a basketball game is only 11.3 points. These are clearly make or break opportunities. Unfortunately, teams have defaulted to breaking.

The free throw is the most challenging technical aspect in basketball. It's more challenging than aspects of most ball-oriented sports out there. It might seem like simple physics, but the physics break in the real world and the ball never sees the basket. This is a discouraging aspect to most coaches and players, but it has motivated me . . . to dig deeper and find a solution.

This book will dive into the problems that players encounter with free throws, why free throws aren't improving, why the typical approach to improving free throws doesn't work, and finally: the one method that does work.

Whether you're a player looking to improve your free throw accuracy, a coach looking to find a good way to teach your players proper free throws, or a basketball enthusiast just curious about why your favorite players can't make a free throw shot to save their lives, this book is for you.

CHAPTER 1

Why Free Throws Are Difficult

The free throw is elusive for players and coaches alike. It's a dreaded part of the game, and one that often lands players a lot of criticism. But what about this simple-seeming shot is so difficult? Turns out, there are a number of reasons. One bigger than all the rest combined is the mental side of the shot.

For one, basketball is unlike other major sports in that it's very fast paced but still requires intense focus and precision. Soccer is also fast paced, as is hockey, but the goals for these sports are much larger than the net is in basketball. This means it doesn't take as much focus to score. In basketball, there needs to be precision to score. Even a fraction of a degree off the shooting angle will result in a miss. When a player has been sprinting up and down the court, their focus honed-in on the ball and their mind making constant checks on the other players, the heart is racing, and their blood is pumping. When they stop that activity to shoot a free-throw shot, their body is thrown out of whack. Free-throws require a calm focus. That focus is hard to achieve when the body is chocked full of adrenaline. Some other reasons behind what makes free-throws so difficult for players are mental clarity and big hands. That's right. A lot of times, it's the post and forwards

that are being asked to make free-throw shots. Players are becoming taller and larger at all positions. Bigger guys or gals, who are tall people have bigger hands. Those hands make it harder to make the shot with the precision required. The same goes for mental clarity. When somebody steps up to the free-throw line, they become hyper-focused on the fact that they're being watched. Their nerves take hold and they become nervous. That negative energy is distracting. The harder the player tries to clear their mind, the further they get pulled into the rabbit hole of nerves.

But anxiety/nerves and the contrast between the speed of the game and the slow-role of the free throw are not to blame. In fact, part of the problem in helping players fix their free throws is that the particular problem for most players is hard to pin down. Everybody fails for a slightly different reason.

A research team made up of economists and finance experts worked together to create a statistical model of free throws to see if they could analyze the data and shed some light on what makes free throws so difficult for players of all ages. They used their financial research backgrounds in application of basketball data to do so by first examining the physical motion of the free throw.

They focused on the major factors of backspin, velocity, angle, deviation from left to right, and height at time of shot. They tried to determine if any single one of these factors was responsible for people missing free throws. Were they shooting to hard? Were their hands placed too high? Were they shooting a little off to the side? This is where the data got foggy. No one physical cause stood out among the others. The results were scattered with all players having variations on the factors in their misses and in their successes.

Maymin, a researcher on the team, said, "The bottom line

result is everybody's problem was different. There's no one thing that everybody is doing wrong. If you look at [Dallas Maverick] Dirk Nowitzki's misses, they're completely different than [New York Knick] Tyson Chandler's misses. It's a completely different thing that needs to be worked on."

Ideally, this information would allow each player to work specifically on what his or her unique flaw was and then the free throw would be perfect. But what the results of the data analysis really showed was that physical factors and variations weren't the real cause. The real cause is mental.

≥70%

mental?

CHAPTER 2

Practice Does Not Make Perfect

If the problem is mental, how do you train it?

Well, most coaches turn to the 'practice makes perfect' method for helping their players overcome the mental challenge that free throws present, as well as use it to help address any technical/physical problems that are regularly present. And don't get me wrong, coaches have their hearts in the right place when they try to help their players increase their free-throw percentage. "Practice, practice, practice!" they say. But practice doesn't always make perfect. For example, if somebody repeatedly squats weight with poor form, the only thing that will be "made" is an injury; which is not synonymous with perfection. The same theory works for free-throws. If a player is practicing with incorrect form or isn't taking the right teachings with them to the actual free-throw line in a game, they're going to cement those bad habits in and their free-throw percentage will never see a meaningful improvement.

Free throws aren't the only case for practice not making perfect. Recently, a meta-analysis of numerous studies about practicing has been done and has found that the phrase is over-simplified at best and outright garbage at worst.

It would be great if practice really did make perfect. That would make a lot of things a lot easier. It makes sense, too, why it would be the case. If you do things enough times, you'll get better at it. That was the commonly-held thought (and still often is). It breaks everything we thought we knew about how the world works if effort doesn't equal success. We're taught that if you put the work in, good things will come. So, it's understandable that it would be difficult for coaches and players to abandon this thought line.

Along the same lines, "doing something for 10,000 hours makes you an expert" is also false. But we cling to the idea that it's true for a few reasons.

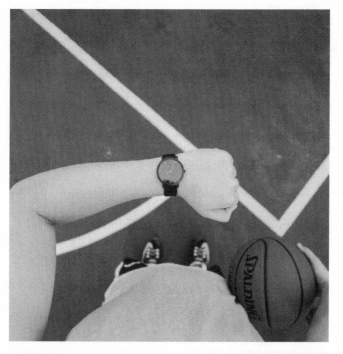

For one, it makes sense that we'd get better at something by doing it again and again. If you cook chicken parmesan 100 times, the 100th attempt will probably taste more refined and delicious than the very first attempt. If you play a song on the piano, after the hundredth time it'll probably sound a lot better than it did the first time.

Another reason we cling to the idea that practice makes perfect is because the idea that somebody achieves excellence without first putting in hard work and a lot of time is really unfair. We roll our eyes at natural talent or people who "have it made" because of this. It breaks our idea of a just and fair world and that's hard to come to grips with. So, we put in our time, we pay our dues, and we work hard to earn our excellence. After all, it has to be for something, right? And if it's not? What kind of world would we live in? Unfortunately, it's not always true that hard work pays off.

I'm sorry to be the bearer of bad news.

The third reason why we're suckers for "practice makes perfect" is because we want to try to force the world to be a more level playing ground. Groups have done this historically when it comes to race and privilege, thinking that if you're born a certain race you're automatically better than another. We do the same thing with those we perceive as being geniuses. If we accept that people are born randomly better off than us, it takes away our motivation to get better. Studies from Carol Dweck, for example, have shown that students will perform better in school, study harder, work harder, and get better grades if they feel it's going to pay off. If we believed that people were just born innately with better chances than us (race/privilege discussion aside), we wouldn't even try to find our true potential or try to improve ourselves. We'd accept ourselves as we are and just wish idly that we were one of the lucky ones.

But the reality is that you can't force something to be true if it's not, even if it feels good to ignore the real truth. That's what this meta-analysis of 88 different studies regarding practice and the payoff from it does. It confronts our idea of success and the road to get there.

15

Some of the authors involved in the analysis, Brooke Macnamara, Frederick Oswald, and David Hambrick said, "The evidence is quite clear that some people do reach an elite level of performance without copious practice, while other people fail to do so despite copious practice."

practice does not make perfect

Their analysis showed that practice is responsible for only 12% of relative success. What that means is that if you practice as much as you can and have all other factors on your side, you'll be as successful as you can possibly be. Without any practice at all, you'll only be 88% successful. 12% isn't a very big motivator, is it?

Those other factors that make up 88% of success are much harder to change, nigh impossible. The research team behind the meta-analysis haven't concluded what exactly those other factors are, but their hypothesis is pretty grim for those who have subscribed to the "practice makes perfect method" and put their stock into it.

The most significant factors that are likely to play a role in your own relative success are:

1. How early on in your life you began that thing you're trying to excel in. If you started playing basketball at 10 years old, you're going to likely be better than somebody who started playing at 15.

2. How well you take criticism and open yourself up to learn. If you're closing off people who are trying to help you and taking their comments personally, it becomes very difficult to progress. Putting your ego aside is good for more than just player-coach and player-player dynamics. It's actually what will make players better players overall.

3. How well you work with others. It's easy to write yourself

competitive

off as better than others, and almost all of us are guilty of doing it in some way shape or form. But if you watch how your teammates play and pay attention to what they do differently that makes them good at certain things, as well as being a good team-player yourself, you're going to become a better player. ~ q k r   r f b ~ s   b ~ d + e ~

4. How much you enjoy what you're doing. If you have passion in what you do, you're always going to have a good attitude towards it. Having a good attitude helps us remember certain things better, helps us learn better, helps us seek out new methods for improving, and overall makes us better people and athletes. The importance of loving what you do can never be understated.

These factors all work together and help boost each other up. For example, if you have a positive attitude because you love basketball, you're likely to be more open to what your coach has to say to critique you because you want to get better. Your love of basketball, in that case, comes before your ego. That's of huge value for when it comes to learning.

Of course, none of this discredits the truth that practice is still important. Practice is where you learn and get critiqued, where you work together as a team under less pressure, and so on. In the case of this chapter, practice refers mostly to doing the same thing over and over. So, you won't learn to be proficient in free throws by just making free throws all day every day. You'll only get, at MOST, 12% better.

Practice is important, as well, for how you feel as a player. When you have more time put in, you feel like you're more capable and ready. Your confidence goes up. Part of the studies that were analyzed for this new collection involved understanding when exactly practice seems to make a strong positive difference. They mainly focused on musicians, but their findings would apply for any type of practice, really. They found that when musicians log their own hours and are self-aware of how much time they were spending practicing a certain thing, they performed 5% better overall. For an already-professional musician, a 5% hike in performance is pretty significant. But this likely just goes back to having a positive attitude. If you're feeling confident in your abilities, you're more likely to have a positive attitude.

The researchers also found that what you're practicing has an effect on how effective the practice is. For example, video games were the most impacted by practice over time. They found that there was a 26% variance in performance between those who practiced regularly and those who didn't. On the opposite end of the scale, there was only a 4% variance for those who practiced and studied hard in college versus those who didn't. Sports falls in the middle at 18%. The factors stated above have a big impact based on the role that they play in their respective activity. For example, college work is much more complicated than video games or sports, and because of that it can be hard to maintain a positive attitude and pure enjoyment of it. That has a huge impact on how well you can remember and process material that you've learned and will be tested on.

Originally, when "practice makes perfect" came to light,

the phrase was never meant to be about mastering a certain task or skill. Practice makes perfect was used to signify the importance of repetition in things like language learning and understanding algorithms. It's for memorization, not learning, not developing a skill. When you're trying to shoot free throws, you're not trying to memorize them. You're trying to develop them. As such, improving free throw percentage will take something other than practice.

Conclusion

CHAPTER 3

The Coaching Problem

Coaches aren't dumb. That's certainly not the issue here. Coaches want their players to win, and they want to do that in the easiest and fastest way they can. So, they focus on easier shots that can be made with more accuracy and improved with practice and simple technique, such as the layup. You can't really blame them for taking this route. The correlation between winning and free-throw percentages isn't really there. Some of the best ranking teams in the NBA, WNBA, and in collegiate sports are sometimes some of the weakest in free throw percentages. Being good at free throws doesn't give you a winning team by itself.

As such, coaches don't put an emphasis on teaching free throws. They don't spend their time trying to find a way to teach free throws. But this creates a need to overcompensate in other areas of scoring. You have to make up for missing free throws by making enough other shots with a decent enough accuracy. By that logic, you're adding more stress to your players by pushing them to work harder to make more shots.

With that logic, you're going to burn your lines out faster than you would if you had a proper balance between free throw shot accuracy and other accuracy. But the problem isn't that coaches aren't willing to work with their team, it's more that coaches assume the problems with free throws rest on the shoulders of the players themselves. The assumption is that to correct free throw accuracy, players just need to practice more on their own time. This isn't correct, as we've gone over, and the correction is more simple than coaches think.

Coaches have an obligation to their team. Their obligation is to teach and focus on helping players to improve. Did you know that on average, players preform 10% less in a game than they do in practice? The major reason behind this is the same as the one that causes free throw percentages to become stagnant: coaches aren't focusing on the mental aspect of the game and not correcting technique.

In order to have players that can get down to business every time they step up to the free-throw line, there needs to be coaches that can deliver on their promise to teach and help players improve. Practice doesn't make much of a difference if players don't have the right foundation to practice upon. Coaches need to know both physical and mental technique, and they need to know how to pass it on. That's why I set out to develop a method that works. I have helped players at every level increase their free-throw percentage and have been widely recognized for my success in doing so. I even had a team that was once voted the best shooting and free-throw shooting team at the University of North Carolina's Women's' Basketball Camp. They don't call me the Mr. Miyagi of free-throw shooting for nothing!

We all want to win. That's a fundamental truth! Winning is our reward for our persistent effort, our pain, our growth, and all the work we've done to achieve that very thing: success. When we lose, we understand that losing is a part of growth. We take our loss and we learn from it so that we may win the next time. But winning isn't always the true goal.

In youth sports, the emphasis weighs heavily on participation of the players and ensuring that they have fun. Still, there's no denying that parents and players alike attend the game with their fingers crossed. Even when participation and fun are paramount, winning is still the goal. Unfortunately, inexperienced coaches use this time in a child's formative years to focus on winning. An important opportunity is missed.

It's not the coach's fault.

There's a problem in how we, in general, approach youth sports. Of course, the primary focus is having a fun, healthy activity for children. But beyond that, we're looking at youth sports with a different lens from what our children are seeing. We're not realizing that our children are in this sport for a reason, for their own reason: they love the sport.

Because we don't realize this, parents and youth sports organizations look at youth basketball with a laid-back lens. They're not employing coaches, they're choosing supervisors; somebody to watch over the kids to make sure everything stays safe and fun. Why not take it a step further? If a group of kids loves basketball, needs supervision, and wants to have fun, it seems like there's an opportunity there that can only benefit them. *Kids have to be focused* *won't work*

The Crucible is my solution to that opportunity. I have listened to what the kids had to say and have seen first-hand the issues that arise when youth sports are treated like supervised recess instead of approached in a real athletic manner. I have pointed out that children reaching more serious levels of sports, like in high school, haven't been taught the necessary foundation of basketball in their youth. This is devastating for children who grow up with a love for basketball. They try out for their high school's team and find out that the sport they grew up playing was a watered-down version of basketball.

quote this.

"This lack of opportunity is very limiting for young aspiring coaches because of the simple fact that youth and middle school coaching is the foundation for athletes' success. Once an athlete gets to the high-school level, if he or she does not have the basic skills and knowledge for the game of basketball, it will become increasingly harder for that kid to continue his or her basketball career."

– Coach Coleman, Bball Crucible

Parents were equally frustrated with this problem. Parents want the best for their children and they want to know they're getting their money's worth when they sign kids up for summer camps and youth sports. They want their kids taken seriously. For the sake of parents and children alike, as well as for the future of basketball, I have set out to solve this problem and help youth organizations change the approach that is commonly taken towards youth sports. I created the Bball Crucible to help enthusiastic parents and youth coaches get a leg-up on effective coaching.

In the program, youth coaches would be trained to become coaches that benefit the kids. They'd focus on winning, yes, but most of all, they'd focus on instilling the foundation that kids need to be able to compete at higher levels in the future, such as in high school. As is said on The Crucible's site, "By the time a coach leaves The Crucible, it is our goal to make sure they have all the tools to instill a solid foundation in every young athlete they come across."

My philosophy comes from a drive to solve an existing problem. My program and I are taking the emphasis off of just winning and having fun and putting it on learning to become good players in a fun, enriching way. The approach is simple: coach the coach and the players will learn the fundamentals of the game. Those fundamentals will stay with them through high school sports and beyond. The players want to be taken seriously, the parents want to be taken seriously, and the sport deserves to be taken seriously. I say, "Let's give everybody what they want" with Bball Crucible.

CHAPTER 4

Mind Over Matter

According to my research, when one shoots a free throw, the action is 10% physical, 20% form, and 70% mental.

Let's break it down.

10% Physical – The physical aspect of free throw shooting has to do with the pure strength needed to get the ball to the basket. Unlike other basketball shots, there is no jumping or any sort of lift to the body, so the shooter has to learn to use their legs as a spring in order to get enough force behind the ball to propel it to the basket. They also have to learn how to make their bodies spring as well to absorb the push from the legs, a coil spring to be exact. The shooter has to get all of his or her energy to move through their body just fast enough as to not fall or go over the free-throw line. It's a delicate balance.

20% Form - Poor form can cause the shooter's body to become misaligned. That misalignment will place the player's joints, muscles and tendons in positions that will cause strains and/or disrupt the trajectory of the ball so that it doesn't line up well enough to go into the basket. The simple free throw shooting position is the player having their shoulders back, their shooting hip (right or left depending on shooting side aligned, and their feet pointed toward the basketball. The elbow should be aligned to the basket. With enough force behind the ball and the form being properly aligned, the ball should go into the basket every time. But it doesn't.

70% Mental – This is where, even if you have perfect form and force, the free throw breaks down. The free throw line is the only place on the court where a player will be totally alone even though they have the basketball. In other places on the court, a player may be alone for a short period of time, but it is safe to say that there are other players that will be joining them to play defense if they have the basketball. All of the pressure is put on that player during their free throw. All eyes are on them. There are a few very different emotions that the player has to deal with simultaneously at that time: loneliness, fear, and knowing that if they miss, the responsibility is on their shoulders alone. theoretically playing

a non team sport like tennis or fencing should help with this anxiety.

70, 20, 10 _ agreed

CHAPTER 5

The Athlete's Brain

Our emotional memories are stored in the central part of brain called the amygdala. The amygdala plays a role in anxiety disorders involving very distinct fears, such as fears of dogs, spiders, or flying. And yes, that includes the fear of shooting free throws.

The hippocampus is the part of the brain that encodes threatening events into memories. So, as a free throw shooter continues to miss their shots their brain will solidify a connection between negative emotions and free throws. Combined with their amygdala playing a role in anxiety, the result will be an anxious reaction every time they come face to face with the free throw line.

During a free throw a shooter is dealing with all types of chemical release in the body. One is the hypothalamus, which controls the fight or flight responses and results in an increased heart rate (which makes it harder to focus or keep proper form). The brain sends a message to the adrenal glands in your torso, which responds to the signal by releasing the hormones of cortisol and adrenaline. That fight or flight response also releases a secretion of glucose into the bloodstream to power you up to get you moving quickly. But when you're standing at a free throw line, you need peace and calm. Not fight or flight.

The brain is the part of the body no one speaks about when they're thinking of athlete health and performance, especially the part of the brain that controls fear. The amygdala

29

is linked to the parts of the brain that govern your senses, muscles and hormones – enabling your body to react quickly to the sight or sound of a threat. The same information can also travel via the cortex, where it is put together to get the whole picture.

The amygdala, an almond-shaped structure in the limbic system, is considered to be the seat of fear in the brain (as well as other emotions). But fear is processed differently than other emotions, bypassing the sensory cortex on its way to the amygdala.

The cerebrum, the cerebellum, and the spinal cord are all connected to the brainstem. The brainstem has three main parts: the midbrain, the pons, and the medulla oblongata. The brain stem controls vital functions of the body, including breathing.

The cerebellum is at the back of the brain, below the cerebrum. It's a lot smaller than the cerebrum at only 1/8 of its size. But it's a very important part of the brain. It controls balance, movement, and coordination (how your muscles work together). Now as I mentioned earlier, on a free throw, the body has to work together as a spring and at the same time keep itself in proper form. If all of these chemicals are being released every time someone is at the free throw line, there is no wonder why free throw shooting is so hard for basketball players and so hard for coaches to teach.

Studies suggest that an imbalance of certain neurotransmitters (chemical messengers in the brain) may contribute to anxiety disorders. Serotonin appears to be specifically important in feelings of well-being, and deficiencies are highly related to anxiety and depression. _i·-ʸ POʋ́+⁴ʲ+_

Serotonin is an oxytocin that acts as an incentive; one of its roles is to encourage us to build trust. A fearful free throw shooter has no trust in their shot and that hurts their ability to make free throws. _bc (ʋⁿfᵢ dↄ+_

So, if the player is not taught how to control their breathing, interpret their memories, manage their fears, and address their loneliness, they will not be a good free throw shooter. Everything from their form and strength to their coil spring action will break down. The ball won't go in the basket. _ʸ(↙+ↄ(_

Research has shown that negative self-talk and anxiety have detrimental effects on players' ability to perform. One study was done in order to examine how self-talk, anxiety, and free throw percentage was related in collegiate basketball players during their games. They surveyed collegiate basketball with questionnaires about their personal information as is related to their demographic, about their anxiety, and about the kind of self-talk they often use (even inadvertently). Then, the researchers took into account each player's free throw record from the previous season.

Overall, the teams surveyed had an average free throw percentage of 66.7% during normal competitions and 60.8% during games that were exceedingly close in score. During close games, players had more anxiety than in normal competitions and the same self-talk levels respectively. This shows on a large scale that greater anxiety, as our understanding of the brain and its role in sports confirms, results in a dramatically lower free throw success rate.

The study also found that the players who indicated that they used positive self-talk methods had higher free throw success rates than their counterparts who used either no self-talk or experienced negative-self talk. The researchers involved proposed that anxiety can be counteracted by positive self-talk, as well as a theory that negative self-talk increases anxiety levels, or even creates it if the player wasn't already anxious to begin with.

This study helps to prove the vitality of a mental approach to coaching and makes the coach's role in helping players with their free throws clear. It proves that practice won't help, and players need to focus on their attitude and mental approach towards free throws. Luckily, the tides are already turning in favor of this new approach. And it all starts with my research.

CHAPTER 6

The Coach Coleman Method

I am a man of many hats. I served in the Marine Corps before retiring to take on a new role of collegiate basketball coaching. I worked with both male and female teams and helped bring my players up to new highs thanks to this unique approach and my dedication to helping them improve at every facet. My last held position in the collegiate basketball world was as a coach and athletic director at the AIB College of Business. Prior to that role, I worked as the head girls' Lady Warriors basketball coach and athletic director at the Northeast Christian Academy out of Kingwood, Texas. During my role as their coach, the Lady Warriors held a 45-18 overall record and had two back-to-back trips in 2011 and 2012 to the Texas Association of Private and Parochial Schools 2A State Tournament, each time making it to the second round. On top of that, the Lady Warriors had three consecutive winning seasons and a San Marcos Texas Tournament Champion title under my coaching.

I also spent 2003-2008 working as the head men's Coyotes basketball coach at Kingwood College. The team visited the Lone Star College Conference Championship in both 2007 and 2008, as well as amassed an impressive 83-58 record.

Aside from those two notable positions, I have had successful coaching positions as coach of the AAU Lady Cardinals from 2005-2010, the men's USS Harlan County team in 1995 (who had an undefeated 16-0 international record), the Hampton Roads NROTC team from 1991-1992, and went on to pioneer various revolutionary coaching programs for youth, coaches, and players of all levels.

My philosophy is "winning is temporary, learning is forever." I take that philosophy with me wherever I go, combining old school techniques of hard work and motivating my teams to be better with new school approaches to coaching the mind and applying new techniques to numerous aspects of the game.

My first-and-foremost approach to basketball coaching is as a teacher. I believe in passing knowledge along and guiding the players to use it properly. My mother was a lifetime educator, so I have seen first-hand the value of education both on and off the court.

I have worked at helping coaches better coach their players. By helping these coaches teach their players how to shoot free-throws, I have single-handedly improved free-throw percentages and win games. With my help, no longer will games be lost at the free-throw line.

The Proof that it Works

In the 2010 TAPPS 2A State Championship game Northeast Christian (Kingwood, Texas) played against, Rockwall Christian (Rowlett, Texas). Northeast Christian won a close contest 50 to 44. The score was not the only thing that was important about that game. What was significant about that game was the point guard was fouled on a three point shot with the game tied. The name of that point guard was Brandon Trower. There was less than a minute on the clock and you could hear all the whispering in the crowd as every person became a sports analysis in the stands. Some saying he only needs to make one, while others swung on the other side of the coin saying he needed to make all three to give his team the lead that would be needed in such a close contest. Regardless of which side a person was on, everyone knew the pressure this young man had to be under stepping up to the free throw line. A shooter feels pressure just by shooting any free throw in a game. Then there is additional pressure put on a player having to make free throws at the end of the game with the game on the line. But this young man had the additional burden of having to shoot these free throws in the last few seconds of the

Texas State Championship game and everyone in the gym knew it. Brandon walked to the free throw line and took a deep breath and knocked down the first shot with no problem. He walks off the free throw line and waits for the referee to walk toward the free throw line. Brandon again lets out a breath of air and knocks down the second shot. He walks away from the line again standing at the top of the circle gathering his thoughts. Brandon meets the referee at the free throw line for the last time. He goes through his free throw routine and takes a deep breathe. He releases the shot and you could hear a pin drop while that shot was in the air. You see everyone can respect the position that he was in. This was the shot that everyone dreams about, but deep down no one ever wants to be put into the position to shoot it.

At the end of the game Brandon and his father discussed the free throws and what he had been feeling. His father said "One of Northeast Christian parents had leaned over to him and asked him if he thought Brandon would make the shots." With confidence his father answered, "Absolutely this was not the first time he has been put in this position." The parent looked taken back by the fathers' answer, but did not say anything else to Mr. Trower. Brandon said "No one but the two of us knew that I had been trained by Coach Coleman and his strange pressure free throw scenarios the last three years." They both chuckled as they walked out to the gym. Later that Spring I spoke to Brandon about his amazing free throws. He thanked me for putting him through those mental exercises. He did admit at times he thought some of the exercises were a little strange, but he trusted me and boy did it pay off. Brandon walked me through every free throw and discussed with me how the things I had him do not only mentally, but also physically. (Walking away from the free throw line and trying to forget about the previous shot and focus completely on the next) He told me that by letting out the deep breathe it helped to slow down his heart rate and control his breathing. He told me he remembered how I told him to imagine that all the fans were pulling for him and to mentally watch the ball go through before the actual shot and so much more. He said everything you told me to do I did. By the book. It was like being in the gym with you and you trying to take away my focus. He said he remembered me saying to him "it is always easier to pass the test if you already know the answers." So I felt I had already done this and all I had to do was repeat it. And that is what I did. For clarification, Brandon Trower had done some one on one basketball training with me for several years prior to him being put into that position.

The other important thing about that game was it was proof that my strange free throw shooting training actually worked even under some of the most intense conditions that a player could be asked to shoot free throws.

CHAPTER 7

The Free Throw Approach

My method of coaching players to better shoot free throws is unique. When I start working with players, I first address their past experiences of failing at the free throw line from an early age. I try to reengineer their brain so that those memories don't come into play in the future.

One of the ways I do that is by trying to distract the player while they're on the free throw line. I have them concentrate on other things, such as technical aspects of form, while they're practicing shooting their free throws.

Then, once the player can keep their bad memories and anxiety out of their free-throw shot, I work on making it a more permanent change by trying to replace those negative emotions with a positive – making successful free-throw. I try to build confidence and comfort at the free throw line by focusing on things like balance and coordination. In essence, I am helping to reprogram their brain so that free throw shooting is a positive, happy experience. Oftentimes, this step doesn't involve a basketball until later stages. Players will practice form, strength, and using their bodies like a coil spring by shooting at objects with a tennis ball.

Another method I employ is to run the players through a series of brain regenerating drills such as right hand versus left hand or right leg versus left leg and having zthem read, think, and clear their mind with regard to past performances at the

think positive

free throw line.

Once I feel they are at a point where they are accepting their new, positive memories and ideas, that's when they go up to the free throw line. Instead of practicing a normal free throw shot, they move closer to the basket to make for an easier, almost guaranteed successful shot. That way, the newest memories of making a free throw are positive ones.

I take that success and slowly start to move the player back step by step so that eventually they're shooting from the real free throw line. Now, it's not so scary. Now, it doesn't induce anxiety. The player believes that they can make the basket, they tell themselves that they'll succeed (positive self-talk), and they make the shot. Now, even if it misses, it doesn't have a negative impact because there are already positive associations in the player's brain with regards to the free throw. They can make shots with more confidence as they are more free and relaxed in their shot, which in turn helps them to be successful in future free throws.

But I don't forget the discrepancy between practice and high-pressure games, so I take a proactive approach to teaching my players to handle that extra pressure in the future. I put the player in different high-pressure free throw situations and walk them through what should be on their mind step by step.

Only from there can the player start to practice the free throw. If they go into practicing the free throw without first reengineering their brains, all the work they do will be fruitless. The free throw is 70% mental, so what needs to be practiced the most is the mental form of free throws. That's exactly what my method gets right.

In Conclusion

Negative or fearful experiences will stick with a person forever if they're not addressed. For instance, if you ask anybody about sharks and whether they want to be in the water with a shark, 99% have never even seen a shark, let alone have been in the water with them. But because of preconceived fears, they do not want to be around sharks. The same situation happens with free throws whether a player has missed their free throw at a game-changing moment that would turn the tides for his or her team, or they've never shot a free throw before. There's still a preconceived fear. →Bad!

Currently and historically, coaching as a whole doesn't tackle the mental aspect of basketball. But basketball, especially the free throw, have extreme mental burdens and if left uncoached, these burdens give ripe opportunities for fear to set in and become preconceived. So, every time a player wants to make an action, their fear will step in before anything else. This results in missed shots, poor passes, bad defensive moves and positions, and low free throw percentages.

The problem rests with and is solved by coaches. I have worked hard on behalf of and with my players to help them become the best they can be by making sure they step on the court with confidence and strength. I am setting an example for coaches through my own methods, and have worked tirelessly helping other coaches improve their own methods and learn new ones so that they can pass their new skills on to the next generation of players from youth level to collegiate. I have done all of this research out of a pure love for the sport, and a drive to see players keep getting better. Always.

References

- Ray Stefani – Four Factors
  http://journals.sagepub.com/doi/abs/10.1260/1
  747-9541.9.2.271
- The individual factors of successful free throw shooting
- https://www.degruyter.com/view/j/jqas.2012.8
  .issue-3/1559-0410.1414/1559-0410.1414.xml
- Relationship between self-talk and free throws
  http://humboldt-
  dspace.calstate.edu/bitstream/handle/2148/164
  4/bobic_andrea_fall2013.pdf?sequence=1
- Importance of free throws
  http://webbut.unitbv.ro/BU2015/Series%20IX/
  BULETIN%20I%20PDF/II-2_OANCEA-
  Study.pdf
- Practice does not make perfect https://osf.io/rhfsk
- James Naismith
  https://en.wikipedia.org/wiki/James_Naismith

Made in the USA
Middletown, DE
09 January 2020